Grandma gave us a dog.
He loved to jump.
We named him Jumper.

Jumper jumped
when we went out.

Jumper jumped when we came back.

Jumper jumped when we played ball.

Then Jumper jumped off the stairs.
Jumper broke his leg.

He wore a cast.
He could not jump.
I was sad.

I took care of Jumper.
I gave Jumper a soft bed.

I put his food and water close to his bed.

I took Jumper
for slow walks.

I took Jumper to the vet.
She took off Jumper's cast.

I was scared.
Would Jumper jump again?

Oh, yes! Jumper jumps when we go out.

Jumper jumps
when we come back.

Jumper jumps
when we play ball.

But Jumper never, ever jumps off the stairs!